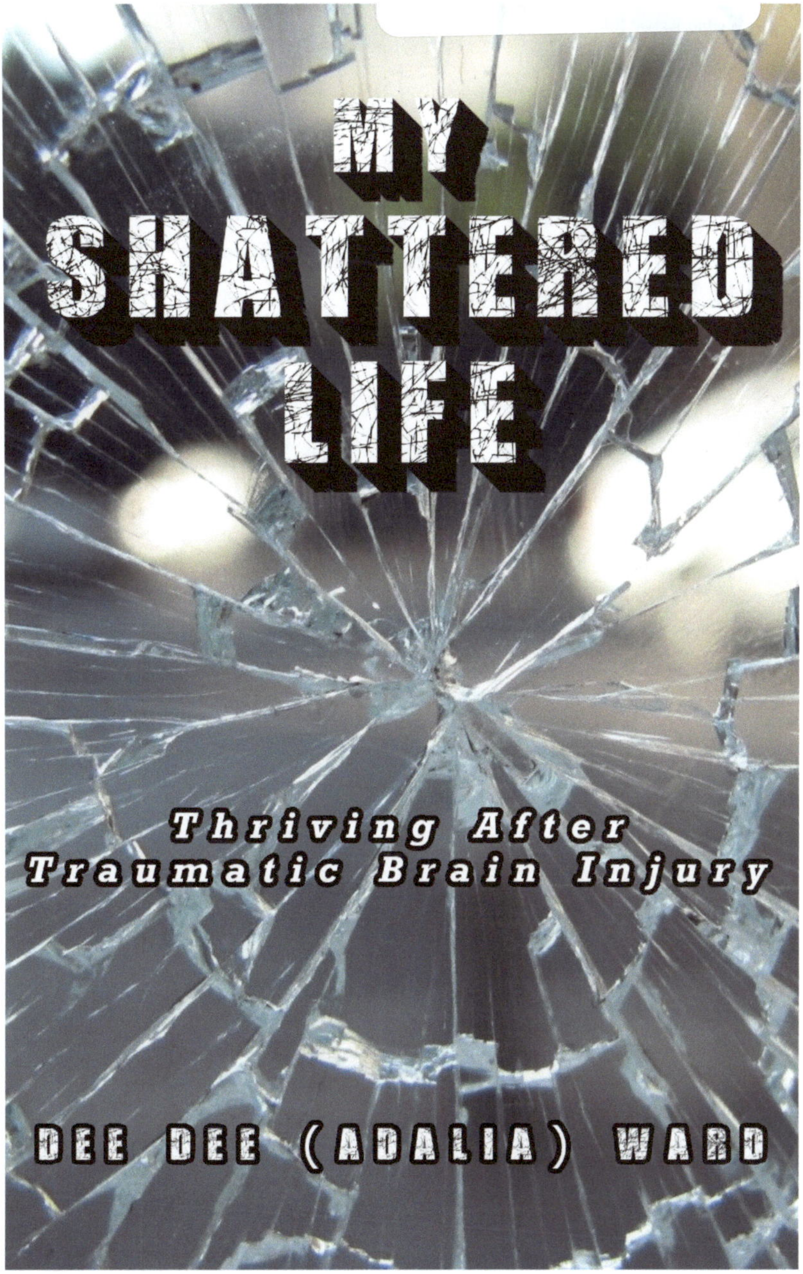

MY SHATTERED LIFE

Thriving After Traumatic Brain Injury

DEE DEE (ADALIA) WARD

Pictures provided by Nikki Pierce—Rustic Spirit Photography, Granbury, TX

(KJV) Copyright ©1976 by Thomas Nelson, Inc., Nashville, Tennessee. Printed in Belgium

(NIV) "Scriptures taken from the HOLY BIBLE, NEW INTERNATIONAL VERSION, Copyright 1973,1978,1984 International Bible Society, Used by permission of Zondervan Bible Publishers."

The TBI Brain Health Groups contributed by – Donna Noorbakhsh, MS, CCC-SLP, CBIS

"Miracle Child" Essential Music Publishing LLC, Sony Music Holdings Subject: Order 387927: License 387927: Approved

Book Cover by Lisa Bell

Paperback ISBN: 979-8-9912639-0-0
E-Book ISBN: 979-8-9912639-1-7
Hard Cover ISBN: 979-8-9912639-2-4

Dedication

This book is dedicated to my miracle son, Andy Ward. He lived, fought, cried, prayed, believed, survived, and was blessed by our great and wonderful Father God. Although he remembers everything from a long time ago, he has no memories of the events included in this book. I often wish God would wipe away my memories of the nightmare we lived. God lifted us up and created new goals and desires for our life. He taught us to be content with the vast changes and move forward from our plans to God's plans for our lives. I love you, Andy.

For I know the plans I have for you, declares the Lord, plans to prosper you and not to harm you, plans to give you hope and a future.

— Jeremiah 29:11 (NIV)

This verse remained on the wall at the head of Andy's bed for seven years.

DEE DEE (ADALIA) WARD

Andy, age 5

Contents

Acknowledgments

A Special Thank You

Lisa Bell, writer and editor, encouraged, taught, and stuck by me during this writing endeavor. Her new book, The SWORD and a Pen: 12 Lessons for Christian Writers, *compelled me to finish writing our story. Her small group setting provided the feedback, discussion, writing skills, and care I needed to complete this project.*

My brother, Johnny Phil Kamp, came every day to help Andy through the months of hospitalization and rehabilitation. His encouragement to Andy was priceless. Phil's humor got us through many tough days.

The nurse at the scene stopped her car on the side of the highway and helped Andy survive. She cleared his mouth of asphalt and stayed by his side until the helicopter transport arrived. An angel of mercy. She also testified at the trial.

Greggory, the doctor friend who postponed his retirement to help us for over a year. We appreciated his medical explanations and advice. He also was a shoulder to cry on. He grew to love Andy.

All the medical professionals at Baylor Rehabilitation in Dallas, Texas, put in a tremendous effort for Andy's survival and for him to have a better chance for recovery.

Sarah, (not her real name) Andy's first true love, waits in Heaven for him. She lost her life in the accident. He speaks of seeing her again one day. God bless her family.

The insurance company listened to me cry and came through for Andy. True, they have rules, but it's possible to break those rules. Readers, please, continue fighting for your loved ones. You are their advocate. It will be worth your full dedication to persist.

Donna Noorbakhsh, MS, CCC-SLP, CBIS, Baylor TBI Brain Health Groups, who promoted our desire to help other TBI patients.

God sent so many angels into our lives during this trying time, which are too many to count.

Thank you all so much!

There are rare people who
will show up at the right
time. Help you through the hard
times and stay into your best times...
Those are the keepers.
—Nausicaa Twila

Introduction

Why I wrote this book:
- God called me to write our story from my heart.

- Lisa Bell taught me how to write better and how to publish.

- Andy encouraged me and demanded I tell our story.

- Researching Traumatic Brain Injuries made me want to write the book and share more information about TBIs.

I have always been so proud to be Andy Ward's Mother. It was such joy giving birth to Andy and watching him become successful at an early age. Both he and I enjoyed lives of goodness, not understanding how quickly everything could change.

We have a testimony to share of how we overcame adversity and held on to hope through our faith in God.

Andy shouldn't be alive—according to the doctors. This is our personal, exhilarating true story of his medical diagnoses.

I started our book in 2020, but I remained too weak to bear the pain a second time. I received another call to complete this book after the twentieth-year anniversary of the accident.

Recovery was slow and steady. We grew content with God's timing and formed beautiful relationships with our Lord. Little did we know, as God sent His angels to guide us through the darkness, their presence was just a glimpse of the miracles yet to come.

This book details our testament to God's power through our bold, believing prayers.

We wish for our amazing readers, walking through devastating times, to please give your situation over to God.

"Pray with authority, boldness, and belief. Bless you all!"

Chapter One

The Good Life

Dee Dee experienced the most wonderful time of her life. May 2003—the years flew by, and for the first time, she lived every day in the present. Today's plans were far beyond her wildest dreams. "I must pinch myself. Is this day for real?" She squealed out loud. "Yippee! It's for real!"

She rushed getting dressed for her wonderfully planned day with Greggory. But this fresh happiness would not last till the end of the day.

In 1996, her pathway led her to a desirable job. Not her lifelong dream job, but a satisfying, good-paying job with a large communications company known all over the world. This global monstrosity provided her enough compensation to live out her dreams. Residing in a historic downtown Dallas loft, among accomplished counterparts who considered her their equal.

Without their knowledge, she led a lifestyle far beyond her means. She allowed herself a few luxuries only when her budget allowed. This fifty-two-year-old woman, mother, divorcee paid the price for this current lifestyle. Two marriages and years of discontentment marked her journey. She did not want to make a bad decision she would regret.

Each day, she offered thanks to God for guiding her through what she perceived as a meaningless life. Being smart—maybe a little above average in the process of aging. She often credited her mom for training her well in performing her night-time routine. Mom understood Dee Dee was not a nighttime person, and she could fall asleep anywhere. Her mom provided the structure needed to perform Dee Dee's facial regimen before her collapse on the sofa in front of the TV each night. This time was presented as bonding time after the hard day her mom always endured.

Through the years, Dee Dee worked hard to make a nice living and did her best as a single mother. Dee Dee raised a fantastic son. He was self-driven and capable of running a profitable company with several employees and remained thankful for their dedication. He attended church regularly and had a kind heart. She had no doubts about his abilities to reach all of his goals in life.

She escaped the small-town lower level of compensation. Her mom passed at sixty-seven, so she wondered how much more time she had on this earth.

All her hard work and preparation had led up to this moment, and she believed it was finally going to be her time to make a mark.

***

Dee Dee exuded excitement, showcasing her attention to Greggory, the emergency room doctor who had become her new dating interest. He treated them extra special that day by planning their attendance at the yearly Byron Nelson Golf Tournament at the famous Four Seasons Hotel & Resort in Irving, Texas. Everyone, who was anyone, was there! Dee Dee had anticipated this event for several weeks prior. She was out of her element but was very familiar with golfing due to her working as a contractor for Head Golf in Ft. Worth. She had learned to play successfully with engineers and doctors and credited herself as a proficient golfer. Greggory and she had played at the famous Camelback Golf Club in Scottsdale, Arizona during a doctor's conference. She had perfected her lengthy drive, but on the green, her ball always managed to pass the hole and ruin her score.

Her clothes were always important to Dee Dee. Her appropriate outfit was a must for her to maintain her confidence in any circumstance. Her attitude was elevated by being escorted by Greggory. His title as a doctor did impress, even though to Dee Dee he was just another man who put on his pants the same way we all do. Plus, he was so passive and gentle.

They joined the crowd and greeted the players as they arrived at the sixteenth hole. Greggory smiled like never before, and she reveled in the moment as they seated themselves on the tuft of grass. His tan and fit physique complemented his tailored clothes, which were in his usual hue of blue. The crowd soon became quiet, and Dee Dee pulled her phone from her cute little purse and turned it off. She would feel so embarrassed if a golfer missed a shot due to her phone ringing. Greggory would never forgive her.

Dee Dee fretfully considered the fresh cut grass a foe to her new green linen trousers and suit jacket as she moved around from an uncomfortable position on the ground. All were awaiting the expected winners of the round to arrive soon. As Greggory was caught up in the scoring, she became unsure of whom she wanted to win. The competitors all seemed so confident and well-mannered as they leaned toward their caddies for the club of choice for their next swing. They attempted to get the small white ball into that tiny hole in the ground. Given the current state of the world, she found it perplexing why this particular game had the potential to be immensely profitable.

Cancer had taken her mother at such an early age. Should we not be paying more for someone to cure cancer or discover a cure for the introduced viruses that were threatening our society? Shouldn't research be our highest paid positions, not sports?

Oh well, she would save those serious thoughts for another day. That day, she enjoyed the lush, fresh cut lawns, the fresh air, and the surrounding finery.

Chapter Two

The Premonition

S uddenly, a tightness in her chest overtook her calmness. Darkness consumed her like an avalanche, sucking the air from her lungs. *"What is happening"* She had never encountered this emotion before.

Move around... breathe...relax.

Oh no! My stomach is in my throat!

Blinking constantly to clear her view from the tears, she whispered to herself.

We need a quick exit. Why am I crying?

What's going on?

"Greggory..."

Was she getting sick from the white wine she sipped earlier in the limo? She had never been a big drinker. Her heart fluttered as she grabbed hold of her purse. "Greggory. Help!" He turned and pressed in closer to her, placing his hand on the small of her back. "Dee Dee, what's wrong?" He wrapped both arms around her. "Are you okay?"

She shook her head, unable to speak.

"Are you sick? Dee Dee, talk to me." His eyes narrowed as he gazed into her face.

"I don't know. I... I... I feel so strange."

Greggory lifted her and guided her away from the crowd. "Let's get you to the car—figure out what's happening."

The couple hurried toward the grand entrance of the grounds. Weakness overcame her. Her legs trembled. Her arms grew numb. Fear tugged at her mind, possibilities screaming.

He whispered kindly, "Stay calm, I've got you."

Greggory tugged, retrieving his cell phone from his pocket. "Driver, please pull the car up to the entrance as quickly as possible. We are leaving." As the driver pulled up, Greggory flung open the back door. They climbed into the calm of the black limousine. He patted her leg as she leaned back against the cold leather seat.

She sluggishly said, "Thanks, we made it. I will be alright. Give me a few minutes."

He looked across at her, and she knew he regretted the fast exit and losing the view of the final round of golf. She'd blown Greggory's plan for a beautiful day.

As the car accelerated and headed down MacArthur Boulevard, Dee Dee could not rid herself of the sensation. Grateful for the rush of cold air hitting her face yet plagued by the dreadful funk that lingered around her.

He passed her a chilled bottled water and insisted she take a sip. "This will hydrate you. Are you feeling better?"

"Not yet." She wondered, *where are we going and what time is it?*

Following the rules, she had turned her phone off during the muted time on the golf course. However, she now desired to turn it back on and check the time. As he watched her struggle with her jacket sleeve, he offered the help she needed. His words were gentle and caring. When Dee Dee pulled one arm out of her suit jacket, the phone fell to the floorboard. Greggory fished around, retrieved the phone, and handed it back to her. At first glance, the brilliant light displays threw her off. The dark tinted windows in the car shielded her from the brightness of the sunny day.

The phone revealed several missed calls. Gen had been calling. Wow—three times. Ben and Gen lived across the street from Andy in Haslet. They left that morning for a motorcycle ride with Andy and Sarah. Her heartbeat increased; dread intensified.

The desperate feelings she suffered for the past half hour came from God! *A true premonition from the Lord.* She never forgot the voicemails that followed.

"Dee Dee, this is Gen! A car hit Andy. He is being air flighted to Parkland Hospital in Dallas. Hurry...it's bad!"

Behold, I have told you before·

Matthew 24:25 (KJV)

Chapter Three

Arriving at the Hospital

G reggory grasped Dee Dee's hand, pulling her through the ER doors at Parkland. At the desk, the receptionist kindly pointed her toward the hallway, insisting she wait there for the chaplain. Fear overtook her entire core as she lay on the cold, damp, and gritty floor. She had no ability to stand. Lifting her head, Dee Dee sensed the wetness of her tears that dotted the stone floor.

Are chaplains responsible for informing you about the loss of your loved ones? Was Andy dead?

She glanced at the clock repeatedly, each minute feeling like an eternity as she waited for what seemed like hours.

Jolted by the tap on her shoulder, the grip on her purse tightened. She looked up at the man standing before her.

"I am the chaplain here at Parkland. Are you Ms. Ward?"

With her eyes fixed on the chaplain's soft facial features, she absorbed the information. Her body slumped down; his arms lifted her. She tried to comprehend the words he spoke. They didn't cross the barrier Dee Dee put up for her defense against the words she feared.

Had he arrived to tell her the worst news?

"Ms. Ward, are you ok? Do you know Sarah? What relationship is she to you?"

Dee Dee became unable to think. She started to sweat, as she replied, "Sarah is my son's fiancé. I was told you could help me. Where is my son?"

"Ms. Ward, I have some bad news concerning Sarah. She did not make it to the hospital. She passed away during the flight."

The cold, harsh words crashed into Dee Dee's mind. She agonized about seeing Andy. Was he gone too?

Sinking to the floor once more, Dee Dee glanced up as a couple approached her from down the hall. The woman held out her arms as if she knew Dee Dee. "Oh my God! Are you Andy's mom?"

They embraced, both on the floor, clinging to each other, sobbing, and gasping for breath. How much more pain could they endure?

No words were needed. Alone in a silence of sorrow only moms could know.

Sarah's mom backed away. Dee Dee released the comforting sensation she experienced as the firm, caring embrace ended. The chaplain led the couple off down the long, cold hallway.

Dee Dee's heart raced. Unclenching her fist, she grabbed for Greggory.

"Oh, Heavenly Father, please help! Where's my Andy?"

With nausea and shivers taking over, she struggled to stand.

"Dee Dee," Greggory cried out, "You must sign these papers. Surgeons are prepared to operate on Andy immediately. I will explain more later." Greggory led her by the shoulders toward two large double doors. "They are trying to save him—please, hon, just sign right here."

Fearful tears streamed down her cheeks. "Surgery? Did she hear right? Maybe a few broken bones.

With a sensation of excitement in her belly, she panted to take in more air.

"He's alive!"

Chapter Four

What Happened?

Hours passed while Andy was in surgery. The hallways filled the outside of the Intensive Care's massive double doors. Andy's motorcycle buddies, friends, neighbors, and family arrived. The news traveled like wildfire. Dee Dee's co-workers arrived, questioning the details of the traumatic accident which occurred that afternoon. She relayed the upsetting dramatic playback of the accident, having received bits and pieces from the police and co-motorcycle riders. Biting her lip, tears spilled with each repeated account.

Four couples rode motorcycles that afternoon, all of them neighbors in Haslet. They reached a red signal light, stopped, waited for the turn indicator, and proceeded to the left. Andy and Sarah drove behind the other three motorcycles on a black, shiny Harley Davidson. An old Oldsmobile pulled out of a Sonic Drive In, going sixty miles per hour containing a man and a woman fighting in the front seat. The man slapped the woman passenger and cursed as she brazenly tossed his burger onto the car floor during their argument. The car accelerated and veered into the turn lane, colliding with Andy's motorcycle.

Andy's and Sarah's heads hit the car's windshield. Both bounced off the car, and their bodies flew face down onto the pavement.

The driver stopped, but did not exit his car after it disintegrated the motorcycle. "I don't want to see dead people," he said.

Dee Dee spewed out a sigh of relief. She could not stop crying, nor form any more words. Greggory took on the task and protected her from repeating the devastating story. All visitors had access to a single-page printed explanation of what happened. She proclaimed him her "hero doctor." He ensured the love and support necessary for her to withstand the "life or death situation at hand."

The police report was not available for a couple of weeks. Bystanders revealed the actual details, and many errors were corrected later. The driver did not have a driver's license, or any insurance, and the car was not registered to anyone. A junker with a hardened man who entered the United States illegally behind the wheel.

***

At the trial, two years later, the driver received a mere two years in prison. The judge's sentence angered the jury members. No restitution. The judge stated, "You can't get blood out of a turnip."

A true statement, but the judge's comments displayed disrespect, especially given the loss of life, severe injuries, and life-altering impact on Andy.

Although he admitted his guilt, the man displayed no remorse. His last words to the jury were, "You all can take care of my three kids while I sit in jail."

The jury foreman declared, "We are already providing for them."

Andy was present in his wheelchair, unaware of what happened during the trial. All the jury members gave him handshakes and hugs while maintaining grimaced faces and shaking their heads in disappointment at the judge's lack of severe sentencing.

On his release, they didn't send the driver back to Mexico. Several years later, authorities charged him with child molestation.

***

Forever admired and loved, amazing men and women, heroes who took part in lifesaving actions, remain dear to the Ward family. Especially the nurse, on her way to work, who cleared Andy's mouth of asphalt and waited with him until the Care Flight helicopter medics arrived. In a literal, selfless act, she saved him from dying on the road.

As Dee Dee reflected on that day, she bent her head and prayed. "Thank God other people stopped their cars and ran to help."

Chapter Five

Learning to Pray

After hours of waiting, the doctors entered the room. Fatigue showed on their grim faces. They maintained an even tone, while talking to Andy's mom. "The surgery relieved the bleeding in the brain. We will follow up monitoring if any further bleeding occurs."

Dee Dee proclaimed horror at the realization of a brain bleed. Everyone knew that's not good. Suddenly, this became super serious again.

Was she in a bad dream? Could this be happening? She was still waiting for the broken bone results.

The doctor continued, "We will refrain from providing any further expectations, because this is a critical time for Andy. We now must wait. I'm sorry. We did all we could. You may want to call in the family." The doctor left, and the nurse escorted them to the private waiting room.

Greggory led her. Dee Dee was dazed. She was in a state of bafflement, and her gaze was clouded.

Her heartbeat became faint. *How could this be happening?*

They entered another cold and minimalistic waiting room. It smelled of despair. The threadbare carpet showed the countless hours of pacing of many family members. The sterile white walls clashed with the worn-out leather chairs.

Dee Dee could not talk to family members and friends as they entered the room and formed the conclusion Andy wouldn't make it. Raw emotions filled the air. Too heart-wrenching. She followed along, but anxiety prevailed. Upon sitting down, she could not sit still. Even though a sudden weakness took over her limbs, she jumped up and ran to the hallway. This couldn't be happening.

Why had she not begged him not to buy the Harley? Why had she always perceived him as being so protected, because he was so careful as a child riding his dirt bikes and dune carts? Never a broken bone, just a few skinned knees, a few sunburns. The favored child with God's hand of protection covering him.

She trembled as two ladies walked toward her. No—they ran toward her. Brenda and her daughter, Tiffany, (two powerful prayer warriors) arrived—just in time. Concern and their sympathetic facial expressions drowned their soft smiles, as they embraced each other in the frigid, sterile hospital corridor.

"Oh, thank you Lord," Dee Dee said. She knew the mother and daughter team from a Bible Study Group she attended at work. "Thanks for coming. Please follow me."

Dee Dee burst into ICU with a strong request for the nurse. Her heart raced as her palms grew clammy with anxiety. Tears flowed. "Please let us in just for a few minutes. I know the rule is for two visitors, but please let us in. Please."

The nurse moved herself out of the doorway without a word. Dee Dee grabbed a step stool, which would bring her up to the side of Andy's bed level. She sobbed and howled, "Please Lord, save him for me. Please. Please!"

Tiffany supported her on the tiny riser by placing both her hands on Dee Dee's lower back. "Dee Dee, why are you begging God? That is not what He wants to hear from you. Pray with authority and in charge of your words to the Lord. He hears your cry. You are proclaiming God's power in saving Andy's life on this earth. Pray with boldness—call out to the Almighty."

"The power of God is incomprehensible to humans." Brenda proclaimed. As she observed the stark contrast, she bravely confronted Andy's damaged appearance and leaned in closer. Then, with much empathy, she asked, "May I anoint Andy?"

Dee Dee's tears continued to flow, and her nose dripped, soaking the front of her blouse. "I am so thankful you are both here with me." Her chin trembled. "Yes, I...I...I need help."

Andy lay in a coma, unrecognizable, head three times the normal size, deep purple radiated from his body. Threads held his pupils in place within shattered eye sockets. Long staples attached his forehead to the top of his skull. Machines flashed alarm lights and beeping sounds, confirming he clung to life.

As she let out a whimper, Dee Dee whispered to God. "How can he recover from this terrible state?"

Dee Dee shared a nod and meaningful eye contact, stood more capable, wiped the wetness from her eyes and nose. "I must not beg—I must pray boldly—I must believe." One scripture reverberated in her mind.

For I am the Lord, your God who takes hold of your right hand and says to you, do not fear; I will help you.

Isaiah 41:13 (NIV)

Chapter Six

Relationship with God

Hours passed and people left the hospital as the darkness crept through the towering glass windowpanes. Distant sirens from emergency vehicles continued sounding. Andy had lived through the surgery. She was right about the broken bones that needed surgery. I missed an important fact that all the broken bones were in his head.

I can't bear the thought of losing him. Her heart was wounded. She wished for comfort. *Would she ever experience happiness again?*

As the hospital staff failed to provide any additional updates about Andy's condition, only a small number of visitors remained, their hearts heavy with sadness. Dee Dee's mental numbness and inability to focus contributed to her lack of responsiveness to visitors, almost catatonic.

She observed friends and family in silent mode, praying privately, with tears forming. Her niece, Emily, displayed her youth at the overwhelming situation. Everyone wanted to help, but they did not know what to say. Dee Dee became concerned that she hoped only to be alone.

Dee Dee listened, with a tightness in her chest, to the instructions Greggory offered. He cleared his throat, rubbed the back of his neck, and prepared to leave. His evening shift at an emergency room in a nearby hospital started soon.

Greggory held Dee Dee tight, hands on both her shoulders as he prepared her for questions to ask the doctors the next morning. "When will they perform the next MRI on Andy? Have the bleeds in his brain stopped? Is he in a medically induced coma or unable to wake up by himself?"

Dee Dee understood and nodded. "I couldn't do this without you."

They had been in a relationship for six months and had developed a strong bond. They traveled well together, and plans were being discussed. Introductions had been made to family and friends.

Witnessing him fade away down the long hallway, she sobbed. With his departure, the silence felt heavy, like a dense fog rolling in and blocking her view. As she retreated inward, she pushed past her limits to find the strength to reassure others. With the aid of a slim, black, tight band, she gathered her long blonde hair into a taut ponytail, straightened the row of buttons on her shirt, and proceeded down the hall.

A nurse, with visible sweat on her forehead, came toward Dee Dee. "The business office on the first floor is ready to release Andy's personal items brought into the emergency room. Can you go now?"

Dee Dee hesitated, then grunted. "Sure." She retreated from the conversation. Frowning, she headed toward the elevator, taking small steps. With pain in her throat, she announced her arrival at the small glass window. "I am Andy Ward's mother, and I came to claim his personal items."

At the end of her sentence, a young lady, with hands trembling, handed her a black leather riding jacket, stained inside and out with dried blood, but still damp in the lining. So much blood. Dee Dee gasped. "Oh no, hon, please dispose of his jacket." She gulped hard and her heart skipped a beat. "Anything else?" She cringed and attempted to escape.

"Here is his wallet, phone, and one envelope." The young lady's voice lowered with each word.

"Thank you so much." Without further questioning, Dee Dee turned around and departed.

She scanned the room, ensuring no one witnessed her receipt of a bulging wallet. Looking down, her hands shook as she considered the crusted blood and wondered what Andy looked like. The envelope, stuffed with money, included a receipt from the sale of one of Andy's flatbed trailers designed to haul multiple motorcycles. Andy mentioned this upcoming sale to her during their phone conversation the day before. He always was so eager to make a profit and wanted Mom to understand he was not gullible and maintained good business sense.

She stopped at the first bathroom to clean some of the blood and store his items in her purse. She glanced around. No one followed her. She even peeked under the stalls to make sure she was alone. She had heard stories concerning this hospital being in an unsafe area. Parkland Hospital was a Level One Trauma Center in downtown Dallas. The hospital's location served as a melting pot of diverse cultures and backgrounds.

Upon returning to the waiting room, her niece, Emily, daughter of her younger brother, Johnny Phil, offered help in bringing her car and proper clothes to the hospital. Emily stayed a few days during the summer with Dee Dee and grew familiar with where she lived. She loved the horse and carriage ride through downtown Dallas one evening with Greggory and her Aunt Dee Dee. But most of all, she expressed, "Best was the shopping trip to Neiman Marcus!" Words could not adequately convey how much Dee Dee treasured Emily's offer to help.

The coldness of the hospital kept Dee Dee in a constant state of shivering. No germ could survive this temperature. Dee Dee would catch a cold with her frozen runny nose. She always held wadded up, used tissues in her hand.

Going through these dreadful circumstances, she longed to immerse herself in her own thoughts. The hospital hallway was enveloped in quietness and loneliness as the last visitors headed home. The tapping of the rain outside gave her a moment of calm. She watched the raindrops trickle down the windowpane. As the night moved into morning, she realized God became all she could rely on. She always prayed and sensed the Holy Spirit in her day-to-day walk. But God wanted more than this mere acquaintance.

You will be secure, because there is hope; you will look about you and take your rest in safety
Job 11:18 (NIV)

***

Dee Dee made it to the next scheduled time to enter the ICU. And the next. And the next.

Then the next.

Andy persisted, clinging to life, but the doctors' reports remained unchanged. Every time, they all said the same words. "A very slim chance of survival."

Broken eye sockets, sliced pancreas, left frontal lobe crushed, and a section of his brain matter above his left eye caught in the fragments of bone at his temple.

A lot of reconstruction would have to be addressed. If he survived.

If? Lord, not if.

The doctors waited until they were certain he could survive another day before discussing plans for additional surgeries. Everyone around her doubted his survival. People asked questions concerning her plans for his funeral.

Dee Dee held tight to her belief God would answer her prayers. She knew God gave her the authority to ask for Andy to remain with her, and He listened. She remained bold and steadfast. God carried her through these dire circumstances. His words convinced her to believe.

Andy always was there for Dee Dee. She idolized her son like a god, and he always remained her constant man-child that loved her. This love would not betray her or remove itself from her life.

Or would it?

She had kept the real God in a second-place position on her importance list.

"Oh God, I've learned! Andy may leave me, but oh, Holy Father, You never will. You are my father, my protector, my healer, my provider, my savior. My everything."

She placed God in His proper place that night. Her genuine relationship with God began the first night at the hospital.

She perceived the envelopment of God's holy arms on the frigid stone floor outside the ICU doors, aware of his golden warmth. She knew the Lord, but the concept of a relationship eluded her. God embraced her, cried with her, listened to her, and adored her. This awareness kept her holding on to hope. As her despair left, she smiled as hope replaced it. She detected it in every part of her body, from head to toe.

Chapter Seven

The Hard Fight

Morning broke out bright and beautiful as the sunshine glowed through the tall windows and the clean, antiseptic smells swirled around her. For a moment she forgot the horror of the previous day. She gazed up at the clock on the wall, then was relieved as she heard the beeping of the monitors hooked to Andy. The familiar sounds lent to her calmness as she was reminded that Andy had survived the night. Hospital staff attended their daily tasks and displayed the busy medical environment.

Could she swoop around the workers to the closest vending machine to silence her demanding desire and need for a diet Coke? It was another ten minutes before her time to see Andy. She would rush. She closed her eyes with the first swallow. Burn took over her morning dry throat. Such gratitude to be given for what she used to take for granted. Her tension released.

Upon her return to Andy's hallway, pleasant thoughts ended. The eldest of the physicians approached Dee Dee as she stumbled back a step or two and read his expression.

"Oh no." She dreaded his words. Bad thoughts raced through her mind as she greeted him but avoided eye contact.

The hard fight began as the doctor faced Dee Dee with the dreadful prognosis.

His voice cracked and his body showed fatigue. "Ms. Ward, Andy will have an extensive recovery due to his condition. He has major damage to his left frontal lobe, which will cause several difficulties to his recovery. This is called a Traumatic Brain Injury (TBI). We will not be able to assess all his damage until he awakens. If he wakes up."

The elevator continued to ding while the worst news possible was being relayed.

If he wakes up! Can I continue with hope?

"Please know we are doing everything possible to provide him comfort and the best outcome." He kept his eyes focused on the hand-held metal file filled with papers.

The doctor continued, looking straight into her tearful eyes. "The first few weeks after a head trauma, swelling and bleeding will affect the function of healthy brain tissue. Andy's eyes may remain closed, and he may not show signs of awareness. As swelling decreases and blood flow improves, so will brain function. We are hoping for him to reach a minimally conscious state where he will respond to commands or show some emotion. Or he may stay in a vegetative state, during which he may briefly orient to visual stimulation and sounds. Try not to become anxious about inconsistent signs of progress. Ups and downs are normal. Let's get this pneumonia under control.

Dee Dee swallowed hard, steadied herself on both feet and sighed. "Will he live?"

The doctor looked up. "Andy has amazed us so far, and we need to move forward in our plan to give him the best chance. He tested for four strains of pneumonia, so we are adding antibiotics as we speak. We believe transferring Andy to Baylor Hospital will be the most beneficial for him. Ask the nurse's station for the expected transfer time. Questions?"

"Is it safe to move him? When and how?" Dee Dee's voice warbled before it steadied. She gazed into Andy's room. Her chest tightened and for a moment she wished she could run away. Instead, she continued saying to herself, *"Everything will be okay."*

The doctor said, "We have arranged for Andy to be taken by ambulance with a medical team accompanying him. We have already set the plan in action but will proceed only if you agree." He paused as he backed against the wall.

He put one hand in his pocket and handed off Andy's chart to the registered nurse as she passed. Do you have any objection?"

"I agree. He has insurance."

The doctor retreated down the hallway. Dee Dee placed her hands over her face and closed her eyes. As a mother, her heart ached.

The nurse informed her everything would be ok. Plans were in action and Baylor prepared for Andy's arrival.

Dee Dee whispered as she walked down the long cold hallway, clutching her shoulder bag. She quickly made a few phone calls to ensure friends and family were updated as the nurses prepared Andy for the move.

She took an elevator down to a parking garage. Now overwhelmed as she looked in one of the many garages at all the levels and cars. She had no clue where to start looking for her car. Due to her distress, she waved over an attendant in a golf cart and asked for help. She gave him a description, license plate number, and keys. As they loaded Andy into the ambulance, the parking attendant pulled her car up to the loading zone. She thanked him with a nice tip and climbed into her car.

"Lord, watch over Andy. Let him know I am close by."

***

Somehow, it seemed as if she was watching a movie while trailing the ambulance in her car. She waited for the scene to change, but it didn't. Her chest heaved as she suffered a deep-seated burst of sobbing. So alone. So scared.

She leaned forward with her hands on the steering wheel. She gripped so tightly her knuckles turned white, and her hands went numb.

"What happened to his future? What will be next? Clinging tightly to hope, she would not let go. She would pray. Her belief would stay strong. But how?

***

Baylor employees welcomed them by setting up all the machines, wires, and contraptions. Many doctors, techs, nurses were on the spot. She hid in the corner, still standing up and quivering. As one-by-one exited, she needed to know. Was Andy ok after the move?

Andy was fortunately not in the Intensive Care Unit. An assigned nurse monitored him through an oversized glass window. As she gazed around the enormous room, with an attached bathroom, a comfy, high-back chair caught her eye. Dee Dee couldn't wait to try it out. Her body sensed the consequences of the strain endured over the last two weeks. She could not remember if she had eaten that day. With a private bathroom, she took advantage of soap and water but did not recognize her reflection in the mirror. The change to her appearance did not matter. She only wished she could change places with Andy.

As daylight disappeared, calmness arrived in the room. She rocked back and forth in her new comfortable chair. She felt powerless, but only for a moment.

"Enough of this. Get up. Andy needs me, and I need him."

She stood and ran to his bedside. The machines flashing and beeping were a constant reminder of the fragility of life. She glanced out the window at the views of the bustling city and lighted skyscrapers. Nothing there changed, but hers and Andy's lives would never be the same.

She bent close to his ear. "It's the two of us again, Andy." She hesitated. "Nope. It's the three of us. God is here." Her hope and strength returned.

***

The unsettled noises in the hospital during the morning were clear. Armed with mops and cleaning products, the cleaning crew entered. The new shift of nurses discussed the evening updates. The RN outside the window shuffled in and informed Dee Dee of the morning agenda of tests planned for Andy that day.

"He has an MRI scheduled for this morning to check brain activity and conduct a full body review for blood clots. The doctor will follow up with a revision of his tracheotomy. This will be a busy day, but we will keep you advised." She spoke quickly as she recorded his current vitals.

Dee Dee asked, "May I follow along with him?"

"Sure, but grab a bite to eat. You need to attend to yourself too, dear."

Dee Dee swallowed hard. "I'm ok. I'm so glad we are here." As she ran her hands through her tangled hair, Dee Dee knew the clock ticking away the hours would test her patience that day—and probably for days to follow.

***

Andy remained comatose. The constant checking of his vitals and rotating his body in the soft sand- and air-filled bed was never bothersome. This special bed kept sores at bay. Vibrating leggings kept the blood flowing through his lower legs. Blood clots remained a big concern.

Dee Dee continued talking to Andy and even made loud noises, held his hand, kissed him, and watched for any movement. To hold on to hope, she relived the fun times, telling him unforgettable memories. Over and over, she told him of their obvious differences.

However, there could never be two people more alike. They both were clean freaks.

With new found energy, she remembered Andy as a small boy going behind her. "Mom, you missed this, and this, and this!" She laughed at the sweet memory.

Suddenly, a nurse walked in and abruptly she lost the good feeling of thinking back to his childhood.

She still hoped he would just wake up like the TV shows always depicted. He'd open his eyes and say, "Hey, Mama. What's going on?" And all would be fine. With that thought, reality hit and hurt like hell.

Two weeks passed with no pertinent improvements. Still trying to conquer the pneumonia and comatose state. The insurance company demanded weekly reports from the physicians. Dee Dee knew recommendations would come soon. They set up a meeting to discuss Andy's progress and review the next steps. She called Greggory, asking for his help. He was always ready and available to bring his expertise to assist Dee Dee. She thanked God daily for sending him for this stage of her life. An angel sent from God.

***

Well after the meeting, Dee Dee realized who would be running the future plans for Andy's recovery. The insurance company held the cards. She knew how to provide the most extended care and the best outcome for Andy. The progress must be noted daily, and the doctor's notes needed to be specific. An additional fight was added to Dee Dee's schedule. She took it on with zest!

Andy moved to Baylor Rehabilitation, across the street from the hospital. The move occurred through an underground tunnel. She tugged at her black pants and faded black pointed collar shirt, showing wear and tear, as she rushed with the speedy techs pushing Andy along the dimly lit tunnel. Her loosened hem in one leg of her pants dragged the floor as they entered a special unit called the Coma Room. In the center of the room was the location of the nurse's station. Five beds partitioned off only by curtains left Dee Dee with no privacy. Andy was the third patient in this vast room. The room filled with transitioning personnel, connecting and securing the functionality of all the machines and sharing information from the hospital.

Dee Dee asked many questions without hesitation. "When will the doctor come? Which nurse is the RN?"

Chilled to the bone, she turned to Andy with a state of exhilaration. "Hang on, Andy. Let's continue to fight."

The doctor, an older woman, showed up in a matter of minutes. Short and stately, with a loud voice, she grabbed Andy's face in her forceful hand and bent low. "Come on Andy! Squeeze my hand." She held his left hand. No response. "OK, but tomorrow, for sure. Let's get this show on the road."

Dee Dee stepped up, leaned forward, and reached out her hand. "I'm Andy's mom." She then focused to listen to the doctor with her head tilted up and alert.

"Well, Mom, let's get your son showing some progress. I will not let pneumonia take this young man. He has fought hard. I will move fast. We will address changes to Andy's tracheotomy, reinserting a new feeding tube, calling in an eye specialist surgeon and a plastic surgeon from Houston, and a pulmonologist. You are in a good place." Her sparkling eyes greeted Dee Dee with strong contact.

"Thank you doctor." Dee Dee took a deep, long breath, letting the new information sink in.

Had the calvary arrived?

As the day continued, the rush dwindled. She dreaded asking the rules of the Coma Room. She had never left Andy since the accident. Would she be able to handle the separation? No personal bathroom for her to brush her teeth or change clothes. She could handle that—even sleep in a waiting room.

The nurse approached her at 9:50 PM and offered a quick smile that faded before she spoke. "Ms. Ward, can I help you with local accommodations? Our visitor hours end at 10:00 PM, but you can return as early as 7:00 AM."

Dee Dee wiggled in the high-back chair and sniffled. Her lips pressed into a tight, flat line. "I've not left Andy since the accident. Are there any exceptions?"

"No, ma'am. We guarantee exceptional care for our patients and will contact you right away regarding any updates. Please get some rest, and we will see you in the morning."

She continued to tap her foot as she dropped her head in disbelief. "I live in downtown Dallas; I can be back here in ten minutes. Let's confirm the number you have for me."

Saying goodnight to Andy was a lengthy process. She could hardly believe the remark that came out of her mouth. "Goodnight baby. Sleep well, and I will be back real early in the morning."

She turned away from his bedside and glanced at the clock. *Was she able to walk away? Would her feet cooperate?*

***

After confirmation of the correct telephone number, she remembered she must find her car again. Still at the hospital across the street. Would she remember where she parked? She hurriedly walked, continuing to hit the key fob to sound her car buzzer, letting her know where she parked. Would she be able to find Main Street coming from Gaston?

Walking through the garage, her heart accelerating, she remembered the cool remark Andy made when she first moved to the loft apartment.

He laughed when she told him she could not find the street of her high-rise building.

The Kirby Building, built 1913, Dallas, Texas

Pegasus Red Horse across from The Kirby Building

"Mom, just look up. Your building is right across the street from the lighted Red Pegasus Horse! Silly, just look up!"

Dee Dee would never forget how he laughed as he said it. Then he added, "Be careful of the one-way streets."

She told everyone that story! And laughed at herself every time.

Her car lights blinked, and she recognized that annoying beep which sounded so comforting tonight. As she climbed behind the wheel, she felt relief as her heart slowed. She locked the doors with the memories of Andy reminding her to do that too.

Driving home after four weeks of spending every minute beside him, she had forgotten how to even maneuver a correct turn. Would she remember how to get in her parking garage? Did she have keys to her apartment? Would she be able to sleep?

She whispered, "Thank goodness I gave my friend Les an extra key. I sure hope he cleaned out the fridge and took my two love birds to his apartment. If not, I'll need to clean all night. "Wow." Her eyes widened. "I can get into clean clothes." Her hygiene was far from priority the past month.

Upon entering the beautiful historic building, she quivered as if she was entering without permission. Everything seemed unfamiliar. Not warm. Not cozy. And not home. The kitchen appeared spotless. No trash, but the smell of the love birds lingered. She checked her phone to make sure she had set the ring volume to the loudest level.

She peeled off the old layer of clothing and vigorously jumped into the refreshing hot shower. "Wow, what we take for granted." She stood beneath the stream of hot water as it filled the small bathroom with steam. Her muscles relaxed.

Minutes passed, then she began shaving the long stiff hair on her legs and underarms. She washed her matted strands of hair, enjoying the softness and creaminess of real conditioner her hair always received in the past. In a swift motion, she dried off and changed into the clothing she planned to wear the next day. No pajamas. She did not use the hair dryer—too loud. She might miss a phone call. Dee Dee jumped into an unfamiliar pillowy bed with no anticipation of sleeping. She wanted to remain prepared to return to Andy at a moment's notice.

But—exhaustion took over and sleep engulfed her.

The hours passed quickly, and morning arrived. As she moved around in her bed, she fought off devastating thoughts. Was it all a terrible dream? Could she wish it away? Why wasn't she angry?

She paused a moment, "Thank you, Lord, Andy is still alive!"

In fifteen minutes, she was out the door and in her car. A contented smile spread across her face. She had avoided any interactions in the hallways that required her to give brief, unenthusiastic responses. It would be too hard to suppress her emotions that morning. She needed to get back to Andy.

***

Johnny Phil, Dee Dee's brother, arrived at 7:10 AM. Fresh from his morning shower, he always had a manly smell and well-groomed air about him. His love was apparent as he remained consistent with his visits. Phil symbolized strength, and she held up well in his presence. He was her favorite brother and Andy always admired him. What he offered was not pity, and it was not what was needed. Many questions flew that morning between the two of them while a pulmonologist and a respiratory therapist assessed Andy. She shared with Phil about the doctor who visited the previous day and her reaction upon seeing Andy for the first time.

Dee Dee explained her reason for renewed strength. "This is the best place for him. We must show progress for the insurance company to continue to pay for his care. This doctor shows knowledge and compassion. She identified with Andy. She cares."

Phil said, "Dee Dee, I sure hope so. I will be here every morning throughout the summer for you and Andy. Expect a long recovery period and maintain your strength. Stay well. Take it slow and steady."

She stood tall, even with a tiny grin on her face to let him know she could do this. She blew out a long breath and smiled. "God will pull us through. He has a new purpose for Andy. He is keeping him alive for a reason."

***

The week went by. And another.

And another.

June and Dee Dee

Dee Dee's dear beautiful friend, June, also lived in a loft in the same high-rise. She came to visit often. June's only son was the same age as Andy. June became the only person willing to help Dee Dee with Andy's needs. Performing diaper changes or suctioning his trachea did not affect her. She teased him later concerning seeing his private parts.

In the Coma Room, patients shared commonalities. Young or old, it didn't matter. Families suffering surrounded them. Lives shattered and changed. Alarms went off, code red declared loudly. Some left, some arrived. Several patients died.

Andy had lost seventy-five pounds total and did not look like himself. His broad shoulders slanted down, and his legs grew so thin. He took several medications for seizures, and God blessed him with none occurring. Dee Dee took over many of the nurse's duties, such as suctioning, emptying his catheter bag, filling his feeding tube, and shaving him. Along with those responsibilities, she kept his small area clean and massaged his arms and legs. The techs seemed pleased when she wanted to learn a new task.

He was so pale and showed no signs of stimulation. His condition seemed hopeless. Friends and family visits became farther apart. Once again, Dee Dee faced the days alone with Andy—and God, who remained beside her comforting, strengthening, and sustaining her.

His doctor stayed steadfast. She called in the calvary.

Houston doctors came. Eye socket repairs with titanium and filling in fat from his butt cheeks to his temples and forehead by a plastic surgeon. Renowned experts handled the massive work.

The results were amazing. The staples were removed, and his eyes rested in their proper position. The areas crushed by the pavement were full again from the added fat removed from his buttocks. Titanium was used to reconstruct many areas of his face. The miraculous art of several talented surgeons. Andy surprised everyone by having all his teeth. Nothing broken in his mouth. Remarkable results. He looked amazing.

They nicknamed him "Butt Face."

"Andy, you're still asleep, but you are looking good."

Chapter Eight

Rehabilitation

Johnny Phil Kamp
Andy Ward
James Ramsey

Life persisted in the coma room as seasons changed. New faces came and went. Vehicle accidents, strokes, and falls brought new patients. Some died, some lived. Life became harsh. Life was so fragile. Some screams of joy when patients awoke; then some screams of pain when others were declared gone.

Dee Dee had a sincere attachment to a young patient who had been t-boned in a car accident. She awoke from her coma, like on TV, and planned to go home. Her parents prepared for the dismissal day. The young lady was a single mom with a four-year-old daughter. Her day never came. She died from a blood clot on the morning of her dismissal. Dee Dee attempted to comfort the parents upon their arrival, which happened just a few minutes after she passed away. They had brought her daughter to the hospital to greet mom that day.

Knowing this event should devastate Dee Dee, she couldn't let it. Andy still clung to life. If she grieved this death, it opened her emotional doors and let in guilt, fear, doubt, and things she didn't dare to feel.

Dee Dee suffered through days that she thought would never end. The chapel was her place of refuge. She was seen many times running, not walking, with her arms swinging all around her body, as she flew herself into the nearest pew to let go of all the worry, pain, and suffering. She then would end in a prayer thanking God for Andy's survival. She'd brush her hair out of her face, and rise with a confident air to her walk back to the coma room to see Andy lying there without a sound.

One Monday morning, Dee Dee heard her brother Phil coming down the hallway, greeting all the nurses, with his cheerful manner. Andy's Uncle Johnny Phil entered the room, approached the bedside, and spoke to Andy first, as usual.

Phil put his finger close to Andy's face and commanded him. "Wake up Andy. Come on."

Andy reached up with his left hand and grabbed Phil's finger.

"Oh, my God Andy. Talk to me." Phil fell across the bed in surprise.

Andy's eyes opened, focused on no one.

Dee Dee ran to the bedside breathless, "Oh baby, it's mom. I love you so much." Tears welled up in her eyes as she strained to hear if he would speak.

A beeping alarm sounded from one monitor and a nurse rushed over.

"Please notify Andy's doctor. He is awake." Dee Dee said as she formed a wide grin.

Andy's eyes continued to blink, showing his confusion. Too much stimulation. He pulled at the wires and tubes all around him. Dee Dee bent low and tried to calm him and restrain his left hand. "Phil, I might need your help. He is so strong." She turned her attention back to Andy. "Baby, you are in a hospital. You are OK. You've been sleeping for a long time."

Phil and Dee Dee smothered him with hugs and tears, wetting his hospital gown.

She wanted to yell to the world, "Andy is awake. This is our Miracle Day!"

***

The doctor brought us back down from our fantastic high. Andy could not follow a command. Room noises were incomprehensible to him. He did not speak. The doctor stated the cold hard facts, but she also noted his awakening as successful progress.

With time, Andy's daily improvements became clear. Dee Dee installed a cork board with pictures of Andy's house, dog, business vans, friends, and family. He still did not speak. He showed anxiety at not being able to move his right side. He had a consistent glaring stare at nothing in particular. No smile appeared when visitors arrived or when looking at pictures of Laycee, his boxer dog. No emotions.

His doctor issued orders for him to start morning and afternoon physical therapy sessions. His equilibrium was off, which made getting him into a wheelchair very difficult. Dee Dee rang for a tech for assistance. He stayed in the coma room for three more weeks, continuing brief sessions with trained rehabilitation techs. They worked with his right paralyzed side while he lay in his bed. Dee Dee performed many of the exercises with him.

Phil came every morning in time for Andy's therapy sessions. He motivated him and the techs to work hard and go beyond normal expectations. It remained difficult for Dee Dee to watch him struggle and cry, due to his insecurities and lack of balance. Phil took a hard stand with Andy to pursue the best results. His use of humor changed the tense circumstances and gave Andy a reason to work hard.

Progress was being noted and given to the insurance company. Dee Dee remained close to the insurance representative who processed Andy's claims. She shed many tears during phone conversations. When more details were needed, the representative advised her, which calmed and assured her of further coverage with compliance.

***

As Andy tried to talk, they added speech therapy to his daily schedule. Maggie, his new therapist, was fantastic and motivated him. Andy reached out with his left arm to greet her as she lingered with her arms wrapped around him. She showed sincere care, and he felt it. She resembled his fiancé who died in the accident. The highlight of his day was undoubtedly his speech therapy session.

He needed to work and learn the timing between breathing and swallowing. He was still reliant on a feeding tube for nourishment. Choking posed a problem. Dee Dee suggested trying his favorite chocolate shake instead of the vanilla yogurt. He never cared for yogurt in the past. It worked.

Andy loved being in his wheelchair, although someone had to push him. He did not understand pushing the wheels himself, and only one side of his body worked. Venturing outside in the courtyard energized his mood for the day. His strong desire to communicate with fellow patients who were sitting outside led us to believe that his motivation would positively impact his progress. His perfect diction excited the doctors.

He did not follow demands, but he sure learned how to give them.

Andy left the coma room for a private room, complete with a bathroom. They removed the catheter and substituted diapers in its place. The room had a significant issue—our first introduction to a single zipper bed. Andy's right side was paralyzed, but his brain did not register that fact. Restraints kept him from a dangerous fall. Unlike in the coma room, where they demanded she go home in the evenings, Dee Dee stayed in his room day and night.

She tried her best to keep the bed unzipped most of the time. She only zipped it up to get food or use the restroom. He used foul language to describe his hate for that bed. This was normal for TBI patients. She was glad something was coming out of his mouth. Regardless of its inappropriateness.

Visitors just had to tolerate it as Dee Dee said, "Please excuse him, but any words are fine with me. For the time being!"

Andy's favorite word became "generator," a sole choice as he struggled to find the right one. A few generators and naughty words would become mixed in. These few words did not affect her revisiting the hurdles leading to this moment.

He later asked, "Why generator?"

"I cannot explain why generator was stuck in your mind. Maybe you were contemplating buying one before your accident."

"Maybe so," he replied.

Andy would scream out, "Mom."

This was the sweetest word she'd ever heard. She giggled. "What son? Here I am!" Energized with excitement, she took a deep cleansing breath.

She was the only person he could identify. He did not recognize any other friends or family, not even his dad. Dickey was a Vietnam veteran and suffered many complications after the war. He possessed two purple hearts. He explained "I can't handle seeing Andy so different. My rage has taken over my mind. I'm not able to come often. I hope you understand."

And, she did understand.

***

Andy took months to relearn colors, shapes, common words to use, and everything. They removed the feeding tube. The risk of falls remained the most dreaded event for a TBI patient. His sense of taste never returned, but it never affected his desire to eat. He gained weight and enjoyed McDonald's hamburgers and chocolate shakes from across the street. The zipper bed came in handy for Dee Dee to retrieve their phone-in order. Andy waited impatiently to examine his delivery. They always got the condiments wrong. Mustard, catsup, and bar-b-cue sauce mistakes almost every time.

"My generator is wrong," Andy screamed, as if it was the end of the world.

Dee Dee laughed. "What do you want? Calm down!" She raced across the room and fetched the large bottles from the storage cabinet. "We have plenty."

His insurance coverage was being strained due to astronomical cost and the length of Andy's rehabilitation. They scheduled a meeting to discuss plans. Greggory was still a dominant influence on Andy's recovery. He spoke to Dee Dee, suggesting an extensive rehabilitation following the Baylor stay. Several nurses mentioned Pate as the best in the area. But the cost? It was a constant fight for his extended rehabilitation and care.

They conducted research and asked dozens of questions. The insurance company sounded promising to comply. Pate would include 24-hour care, with several therapy sessions daily. They could choose from two locations. They opted for Irving, TX, not too far from Dallas.

Doctors suggested placing Andy in a nursing home instead. They offered Dee Dee a list of names and locations. Early the next morning, while Phil was with Andy, she jumped in her car and loaded her GPS with one name and address on the list. She drove about three blocks.

"What the heck am I doing?" She made an illegal U-turn without checking for safety. She suppressed her anger by taking it out on the leather steering wheel. She yelled at herself. "Concentrate on arriving back at the hospital in one piece.

"No way am I considering this suggestion. Pate is our chosen option. Andy needs the insurance to come through." With a wide grin, she went back and caressed Andy.

God was so good. He brought Andy so far, surely, He would take care of putting Andy in the best possible place for recovery.

***

Pate was the answer to their prayers. Greggory gave Dee Dee his admired remark, "Good job," over the phone.

During the day, Dee Dee worked from 7:00 AM until 4:00 PM, and at night, she slept in Andy's new room. The therapists worked Andy vigorously. His speech and thought processes improved. His vacant gaze remained, yet Dee Dee sensed he comprehended the words spoken to him.

Despite Andy's progress, he needed someone to make decisions for him. The legal process for Dee Dee to become Andy's guardian was underway. They required separate legal representation. She gritted her teeth opening the invoices for the legal fees. Andy's business, home, vehicles, and employees needed attention. Andy, at only 29, had not planned for Mom to step in and manage his accounts. They did everything the legal way, even though others gave them all kinds of workarounds. Dee Dee knew Andy would desire her to do it right, through the court system.

The weeks and months flew by. All the holidays were just another day. The well-trained staff remained vigilant. The surroundings were well-maintained, bright and sunny, and created an uplifting ambiance.

Ten months passed. Dee Dee continued working with the insurance company, and they continued paying. Andy's improvements remained celebrated royally by the energetic young staff.

Andy referred to his therapy sessions as celebrations. "How many parties am I going to today?"

They ordered an electric wheelchair, but its approval was pending. Thirteen thousand dollars seemed farfetched. Other medical supplies for home arrived.

Time ticked away toward dismissal. The insurance company would decide the exact day. It had been well over two years, and Dee Dee only knew that home was wherever Andy was.

Chapter Nine

Home at Last

Home. An apartment in a high-rise in downtown Dallas, known as the Kirby building. Fifteenth floor. Built in 1913 with seventeen floors, the late Gothic Revival tower was one of the most distinguished landmarks. Residents experienced a connection to the past with original hardwood floors, exposed brick, and vaulted ceilings. Dee Dee enjoyed the expansive city and skyline views. She worked across the street in another high-rise building on the eighth floor. Channel 4 TV had filmed a special, featuring Dee Dee, her loft, and the convenience of living and working in downtown Dallas.

Andy's home in Haslet, about forty-three miles away, was on the market to sell. To ensure Andy's safety in the new environment, the apartment needed extensive changes. A new lower bed installed, rugs removed, and furniture eliminated to clear walkways. Medical supplies included a shower chair, walker, recliner, and bed rails, all unboxed and ready for use.

Dee Dee contacted a health care service company to hire a home assistant to stay with Andy during her work hours. She planned to come home every day for lunch to check on Andy. God placed her in a perfect location.

She always wondered why she was willing to make her home here. She had been commuting from a beautiful custom-built home that she designed, on ten acres with a nice pool sixty-five miles away in a country setting near Richland Chambers Lake. She was ready to get off of the interstate and enjoy some conveniences. Yard work had worn her down. The thought of walking to work and getting home before dark seemed like her dream had come true.

A loft proved larger for the new add-ins for Andy's care. Dee Dee always put much effort into making her home beautiful, but these medical items didn't help the aesthetics. She strained to accept and embrace the unfamiliar decor, determined to find contentment.

Dee Dee often said, "What would Channel 4 think about my apartment's new look?"

It didn't matter. Andy was coming home. She'd prayed long and hard for this day. Had the hard fight ended? Would she be overprotective? Many questions and disturbing thoughts troubled her mind. Worrying was not the answer. She could persevere—with God's help. Without Him, she'd fall apart.

Dee Dee cried in private while she suffered with headaches and stomach issues. She never let Andy see any of her discomfort. How would she handle this new transition?

She told her friend June, "No one else will ever hear of my doubts. I firmly rejected any other options, and always will. I will bring Andy home, and it's my final decision."

June agreed.

Dee Dee trained to get Andy in the car for the trip home. Step-by-step. That morning, she bounced into Andy's room. "You're going home today, Andy."

His empty stare haunted Dee Dee as she repeated the plan for the day. "We're going home. I'm so excited. Are you excited too?"

No answer.

Uncertain if he understood the significance of the day, she grinned exuberantly at him.

"Andy, this day has finally arrived, and Mom is so happy."

As she pulled out onto MacArthur Boulevard, he repeated several times, "Wrong way."

"New home, Andy. We are going downtown, close to the hospital. Mom's home. It's ready for us." She glanced over at him with amazement, he noted they were not headed toward Haslet, his house.

They arrived in the parking garage of her high-rise, and the test started. Her assigned space was on an extreme slant. She unfolded his wheelchair and lifted him out of the car into the chair. Success! He was in. She turned to pull out an overnight bag.

Movement unexpectedly caught her eye. She glanced toward Andy. "Oh, my God!"

His chair rolled down the hill and headed for a brick wall. Had she forgotten to set the brake? She turned and screamed frantically.

"Andy, I'm coming!"

His head tilted back as the wheelchair picked up speed.

She ran after the chair. If he got hurt, she would blame herself forever. Terrible scenarios flashed through her mind as she sprinted after him, almost tumbling down the concrete toward the wall.

"Oh Lord, what have I done?" The cool air met her damp blouse and gave her a little boost to run faster. Would she see red? Blood?

Andy laughed as he stuck out his left leg to protect himself from the impact. Dee Dee caught up and looked him over.

Andy cocked his head. "Why are you crying? I'm OK."

"Are you sure you're alright?" She gulped hard and kissed the top of his head.

She looked back to the car, the overnight bag thrown beside it. Did she have enough strength to push his wheelchair up the incline? Wobbly knees, and pushing with all her might, her legs trembled and threatened to give out. Only with God's help would she make it. Andy continued to grin and laugh, as if he had a joyful ride at an amusement park.

Dee Dee always hid her frustration from Andy to keep him calm. And in that moment, she thanked God she had to push him from behind. The tears continued streaming down her cheeks as she panted up the incline.

Nearing the car, she stopped crying and caught her breath. "All is OK. And I've got another hilarious story to share with everyone later."

Andy just laughed more.

***

Every day, new challenges arose. She pleaded with management for a safer parking spot on the first floor. Management assigned the best parking to penthouse tenants.

She didn't give up and reminded staff and others in the building. "This could be one of you someday."

They hesitated, then later gave in to her request after three intense meetings. Their stubbornness taught Dee Dee to never give up.

Out-patient rehabilitation at Baylor was critical, five days a week. His aid assisted him, and Baylor provided the transportation, a nice wheelchair accessible van. Adjustments to various braces continued to be essential in his ability to walk. Andy had the tendency to walk on his heel, without flattening his foot. This remained a severe problem. They explained his brain did not know the position of his right foot. Blisters and sores hindered his progress to walk. The braces proved to be more trouble than help. Surgery on his right foot finally took place. He endured a cast for six months with no notable results. They both endured a tough hot summer.

The aids the Health Services sent were not always up to her standards. The happiest, well-dressed, older lady, who seemed so perfect, revealed why she maintained her jovial personality all day. Dee Dee noticed the decrease in the vodka bottle kept in the freezer. She marked the bottle with a black marker and observed the daily consumption.

Soon she confronted the lady, and she admitted her offense. "Well, I have a minor drinking problem."

Dee Dee crossed her arms, and glared at the woman, "Well, I have a major problem with your drinking while taking care of my son."

Health Services replaced her.

Any aids that were smokers left him often to visit the rooftop. Dee Dee showed Andy how to call her when he knew the aids neglected him. Through many aides, they remained displeased with the caregivers. The company advised her to recommend a friend or relative they could employ through their service. Perfect solution. They reached out to a retired gentleman. James was married to Brenda, who taught Dee Dee how to pray that first night at the hospital. She and her husband, James, had stayed in touch. How fitting that James could become Andy's caregiver. And Dee Dee had no doubt he'd take great care of Andy. James got him out of the house. Fishing, garage sales, and playing pool gave Andy a reason to wake up and get dressed.

In the early mornings, James strolled in, calling out to Andy. "Make sure you're dressed and ready for a fun day! How about Dave & Buster's?"

Andy yelled back. "I stay ready, James."

James always grabbed a few extra adult diapers and Andy's medicine. He remained a blessing for several years. Another reason for Andy's progress.

Months passed. Dee Dee's friends at work and June played a big part in looking after them. Meals and visitors poured into the apartment. She enjoyed every minute with Andy. He loved playing checkers and several simple board games.

When Andy was young, they always baked chocolate-chip cookies before bedtime. This routine continued during his recovery. With one minor issue. Andy would eat about twelve cookies and wash them down with an oversized glass of milk, then go to bed. With his loss of memory, Mom learned quickly not to clean up the kitchen. In about ten minutes, Andy said, "Let's make some cookies." One night, they baked and consumed three batches of cookies.

Dee Dee shrugged and said, "Oh well, he needed to gain weight."

Word search books kept him occupied. He took seventeen pills each day to control his moods and frustrations.

They worked.

The persistent problem of Andy's short-term memory loss continued to be a significant concern. Eraser boards, printed calendars, Apple watches, and cell phones helped overcome the complications. Even though Andy could not taste food, his meals dominated his daily routine. He often asked if he had already eaten.

"Hey, Mom. When is dinner?"

She laughed under her breath, remembering the night of multiple batches of cookies. "Well, Andy, didn't you enjoy the steak, baked potato, and salad we ate about thirty minutes ago? But if you're still hungry, I will be glad to make you a sandwich."

"A sandwich?" Andy wrinkled his forehead. "Are you sure?"

Dee Dee tried to pull this joke on him when she didn't want to cook. It lightened the seriousness and checked his memory. It worked—for a while. He finally caught on to her. No steak and baked potato earlier, and he refused to settle for a sandwich.

Dee Dee realized the convenient living location for work was no longer suitable for them. James endured a lengthy drive, and Andy insisted on getting a new dog. Laycee had died of old age while Andy was in the hospital. The need for a yard became clear.

Four months before his out-patient rehabilitation was scheduled to end, she found an empty lot next door to a friend and co-worker. Then she contracted the building of a new wheelchair-accessible home with an older Christian builder. He favored Andy and provided an exceptional, affordable home.

***

The move proved to be the worst physical endeavor Dee Dee ever survived. Andy's furniture and belongings were kept in storage after selling his home, and she underestimated the amount that needed screening. His business painting tools and supplies remained in storage. She was overwhelmed by the amount of the deliveries which exceeded the capacity of the new home. Andy found solace with a neighbor until the establishment of security and stability in the new residence.

The fenced back yard provided Andy with hours of enjoyment. Smooth sidewalks enabled him to reach a five-acre pond facing their back property. The covered patio provided him shade. The design kept Andy's safety in mind, enabling him to maneuver around in his electric wheelchair. If it ever arrived!

The home had wide doors, safety bars, no steps, and a large game room tailored for Andy. A pool table would arrive soon. Mom stated the reason for the purchase of the pool table. "Now Andy, you must stand to make shots on your pool table. Raise yourself out of your wheelchair." This proved to be a great incentive.

Andy remained confused in the new home. He searched for his bathroom and roamed around the house, searching for his books and even his recliner.

Andy never asked for help. He maneuvered his push-style wheelchair like a pro. He persisted in covering for his confusion in the new surroundings. More thinking. More frustration.

"Mom, they laid out this floor plan so poorly. I could have done better in my sleep." He often let out a slight laugh when he said this.

Adhering to a routine kept Andy from experiencing too much confusion. Changes to his routine caused him to say things without a filter, not caring who listened. He told her often "Please slow down. I can't do this."

His English bulldog, Bully, which Mom purchased before the house was finished—a big mistake. Bully had to be trained to use his new doggy door. This became an urgent necessity. They pushed this fifty-four-pound gentle giant through his door several times. Success! He became the baby in the family. Bully was as confused as Andy.

Thank goodness Dee Dee took a week of vacation for the move. She struggled to walk the next two days. Taking Tylenol regularly helped with the severe pains in her shoulders, legs, and feet. Boxes needed to be emptied. Andy couldn't, so she did the work. With boxes finally unpacked, despite the pain, Dee Dee collapsed on the sofa.

Home at last.

From Paul to the Apostles: "And my God will meet all your needs according to his glorious riches in Christ Jesus."
— Philippians 4:19 (NIV)

Chapter Ten

Striving for Contentment

Dee Dee's plans for her future changed. She dedicated her life to caretaking. She admitted, "Andy also takes care of me."

Financial decisions needed to be made, not only to care for her retirement, but also for Andy's lifetime. God continued to boost her career and build her 401K contributions. She secured life insurance policies outside of the company where she worked. They offered a 100% company contributed pension. She met her goals for their future, according to her financial advisors.

Andy's plans for his future changed. For the rest of his life, he would live with his mother. He lost his marriage plans. He would need assistance to live a somewhat normal life.

His relationships with his two little nephews, Abel, and Luke Epperson, Emily's boys, grew deeper every visit. They brought Andy a special love that deepened with sincere hugs and grins.

Luke, Andy, Abel, and Emily

All the doctors said, "Andy will become depressed and will need counseling."

Test had proven, depression has never happened.

Dee Dee worked through the stress concerning Andy's future when she passes away. She tailored an agreement with her niece, Emily, to be his future advocate and manage his finances. The accident did not affect Andy's level of maturity;

therefore, he could assist in decision making. As a team, they ensured his well-being through trust-fund arrangements.

When asked by others, Dee Dee said, "God has watched over Andy all along, and He will continue when I go home to Heaven."

***

A new wonderful church welcomed them with open arms. The congregation prayed, laid hands-on Andy for healing, and allowed them to enjoy an extended family. Their new home granted Andy newfound freedom. Progress continued in his recovery.

The key to their happiness could only come by achieving contentment with their new lives. God used his eraser on their plans. He replaced many worldly goals with heavenly goals. Dee Dee had to let go of her strong, successful business-owner son and accept her new handicapped, struggling son. Her friends had to listen repeatedly to the same stories as she required their patience.

This was a deep and painful grieving period for the old Andy, but she accepted the new Andy with a lightness in her chest. This phase lasted for two years of hard work, tears, and countless prayers to find contentment and joy again. Grief takes time, and they had to grieve their losses before moving forward.

"We both felt God's hands on our daily walk. We reveled in the simplicity of our new lives. Now calm and fearless."

Andy rushed to give his testimony to anyone who would listen. He relished opportunities to talk or engage with others and became a powerful prayer warrior. A miracle child, he became more like Jesus every day.

They achieved contentment.

Chapter Eleven

God's Timing

Day-by-day, hour-by-hour, minute-by-minute. Andy continued to improve. Years passed.

Progress was slow, so slow. Dee Dee smiled every day as the progress became clear.

Prayers went up. God answered those prayers. Andy, Dee Dee, friends, family, coworkers and church members all praised the Lord.

Andy's short-term memory never returned. He dressed, not remembering if it was summer or winter. Mom explained, "A heavy sweater with his flannel pajama bottoms did not work for a 105-degree day in Texas."

His medications being taken, became a must. He could not taste his food. His hearing was five times normal hearing, which made ear plugs necessary. He continued suffering with sores on his feet, trying to walk in the seven different braces that never improved his gait.

The electric wheelchair finally arrived. Andy's Medicare and Medicaid were activated and covered medical bills. Texas benefits paid for his daily aide. Andy's SSDI deposits helped tremendously. The Guardianship completed with the court and was stamped, paid in full.

God blessed them from all directions.

God was so good.

Not our timing, His timing.

***

One morning, after seven years, Dee Dee scrutinized Andy. She leaned in, with intense concentration upon Andy's face. "How are you today?

He appeared vibrant, no fixed stare into nothing. "I feel great Mom!" He looked into her face, her eyes. He was present.

Aware of his clear speech and radiant eyes, she asked. "What, no more generators?"

He waved his arms and became demonstrative, ignoring her question. "What? What are the plans today, Mom? It's Saturday. Let's do something fun."

"My miracle child, with God's timing. Not our timing."

But those who hope in the Lord will renew their strength. They will soar on wings like eagles; they will run and not grow weary; they will walk and not be faint.
— Isaiah 40:31(NIV)

For the revelation awaits an appointed time; it speaks of the end and will not prove false. Though it lingers, wait for it; it will certainly come and will not delay.
— Habakkuk 2:3 (NIV)

This verse tells us God has a special time for everything. Even if His plan seems slow, we must be patient because it will surely happen at the right moment. God communicates with Habakkuk in this Bible verse regarding what lies ahead.

It reminds us to trust in Him during our waiting periods. The message here is clear—believe He controls all things, and His timing makes every event beautiful in its own way.

Chapter Twelve

How Life Changed

Andy copes with typical physical and emotional difficulties following a TBI.

- No short-term memory. Major issue. He cannot make any new memories. A critical issue for taking his medications, conversations, and forming relationships.

- Poor blood flow in his legs causes the need for vein surgeries. He had four surgeries.

- His eye damage causes frequent cataract surgeries. He had one removed.

- Encountering challenges with mobility. His balance proves to be detrimental to his safety.

- No sense of taste.

- Emotional outbursts.

- Frustrations.

- Lack of patience.

- Difficulty with others entering his personal space. Walmart trips are limited.

- Cannot tolerate loud noises. Ear plugs are necessary.

- Needs constant help.

***

Andy started working at fourteen. Everyone thought he wanted to become a banker, because he loved to count his money. He started working for a neighbor who owned a painting business when he was only sixteen. At nineteen Andy owned his own paint contracting business, employed several full-time employees and many part-time. He achieved remarkable success in handling apartment contracts, new construction projects, working with designers, and securing commercial accounts. He expressed immense gratitude for his exceptional employees and clients. At only 29, his world changed.

***

Dee Dee raised Andy emphasizing the importance of striving for perfection in life. She tried to set an example. He fought hard to reach the worldly view of perfection. Good job, beautiful home, big new cars, successful friends, and a beautiful fiancée.

What a mistake—for both him and her.

What have we learned?

- Perfection is a worldly goal.

- Perfection is not a godly goal.

- God did not use perfect people for his works—except for Jesus.

- We don't need to be perfect.

- We are to give our testimony.

- God receives all the glory.

Hudson Taylor, a British missionary in China in the 19th century, once said,

"All God's giants have been weak people."

You can see the truth of that statement throughout the Bible. God loves to use weak people to fulfill his will.

We all write our plans in pencil. God takes His eraser and changes those plans. Lives are sometimes shattered—we think! But God never gives us more than we can handle. Imagine... we can achieve profound satisfaction and contentment despite horrendous life changes. We are proof of this.

Andy 29, 2002, before accident

One day you will tell
Your story
Of how you overcame
What you went through
And it will become someone
Else's survival guide
—Brene' Brown

Chapter Thirteen

Thanks to God

A ndy and Dee Dee's Prayer

Our hearts overflow with gratitude as we witness your miraculous works in Andy's life, Lord.
We exalt your name and share our testimony with everyone.
Thank you for your goodness. We praise you, Father God.
In Jesus' name.

Amen.

***

Give thanks to the Lord, for he is good, His love endures forever.

— Psalm 86:10 (KJV)

For thou art great, and doest wondrous things:
thou art God alone.
— Psalm 86:10 (KJV)

"Jesus is the miracle worker. He can transfigure and transform. He can work the miracle of a new birth for you so that you have spiritual life that is eternal."—Written by Hoyt Wilson, Pastor, First Baptist Church, Lexington, Tennessee. Our blessings continued with new friends. We called them our angels. Our church family filled our hearts with joy and gratitude. We opened our home for church groups to meet and enjoy.

***

A new promotion at work for Dee Dee relieved the financial strain and secured her ability to remain in a stable position with the company until retirement at age sixty-nine.

As time passed, Andy laughed with less confusion and enjoyed many extra activities. As he explained his lack of memory, he always asked if a person had ever seen the movie, *Fifty-First Dates* with Adam Sandler and Drew Barrymore.

People commonly said, "Yes. Are you ten-second Tom?"

He joyfully replied, "No, I'm one-hour Andy."

Dee Dee always chimed in, "It is great. When he gets aggravated at me, he gets over it in about an hour. We try to turn the situation into a blessing."

We both learned how to laugh again.

Chapter Fourteen

TBI Brain Health Groups

The Brain Health Group motto is: "Starting today, I will acknowledge what is gone, appreciate what still remains, and look forward to what is coming next."

– Donna Noorbakhsh, MS, CCC-SLP, CBIS

This motto is one that still rings true today.

A special thank you to Donna Noorbakhsh who is a licensed Speech Language Pathologist and Certified Brain Injury Specialist with Baylor Scott and White. Her Brain Health Group provided critical information that Andy and I needed to understand the changes that we were living.

Andy and I valued our time during these many sessions and learned new skills to handle our difficult situations.

Donna's TBI support group was designed to provide on-going support to individuals living with TBI across the DFW area. She met individuals of all ages, each of whom were seeking support and education after their traumatic brain injury. She aspired to educate, support, and create a brain healthy community for individuals living with TBI.

Her focus was to provide support and education to individuals living with traumatic brain injury through instructional sessions, group discussions, and structured tasks geared toward improving mental well-being and quality of life.

***

Objectives of the Brain Health Group included:
1. Having a better understanding of traumatic brain injuries and how they impact physical, cognitive, and mental well-being.

2. Learning strategies to manage and improve anxiety, depression, fatigue, and cognitive functioning.

3. Learning how to take control of your brain and improve your brain health.

4. Developing and working toward individualized short-term and long-term goals aimed to improve brain health and quality of life.

The participants in this group learned about factors that influence brain health and could improve the brain's functioning after a traumatic brain injury. In this group, participants learned to appreciate, protect, and nourish the brain with knowledge, nutrition and self-love. By implementing this practice, participants were on a journey toward a healthier brain - and a healthy brain is a happy brain.

Support groups are valuable for a multitude of reasons. They provide a safe and non-judgmental environment in which individuals can share their feelings and experiences. Members of a support group often engage in more candid discussions relating to sensitive topics such as intimacy, drugs, alcohol, and other areas of daily life without fear of being judged or misunderstood. Furthermore, these groups allow survivors to share advice regarding their experiences, resources, and offer peer support.

***

"One thing I fondly remember about Andy is his genuine smile which can only be described as contagious! Anyone who spends time with Andy will inevitably be grinning from ear to ear by the time they leave due to his jovial personality and jokes. Even when we were discussing serious topics, he would find a way to make everyone laugh and remind them of the joys in everyday life. When group members felt discouraged, Andy would be the first to lift them up and encourage expressing gratitude. Andy served as a role model to others and continues to positively influence individuals living with TBI." –

Donna Noorbakhsh, MS, CCC-SLP, CBIS

Chapter Fifteen
Miracle Child

This is our favorite song.

"Miracle Child"

Words of Song—Sang by Brandon Lake

I shouldn't be alive

My future was six feet under

One foot in the grave

No hope to be saved, yeah

I shouldn't be alive

But I'm a miracle child

Defied every diagnosis

And as close as it came

I can stand here and say

I'm a miracle child

Death, where is your sting?

My Savior's word is final

I am resurrected

Blood protected
I am a miracle child
If you're facing the odds
If you think you're beyond His saving
There's no life He can't raise
No, your wounds aren't too great
He's a miracle God
Cause He shouldn't be alive
His body was six feet under
Three days in the grave
But that stone rolled away
Yeah, our God is alive, oh
Death, where is your sting?
My Savior's word is final
I am resurrected
Blood-protected
I am a miracle child
Oh, death, where is your sting?
My Savior's word is final
I am resurrected
Blood-protected
I am a miracle child
Oh, death, where is you sting?
My Savior's word is final
I am resurrected
Blood-protected
I am a miracle child
You're the living, breathing God of glory
I'm a living, breathing testimony
You're the one who turns a dead-end story

To a living, breathing testimony
You're the one who turns a dead-end story
To a living, breathing testimony
Death, where is your sting?
Cause my Savior's word is final
I am resurrected
Blood-protected
I am a miracle child
Oh, death, where is your sting?
My Savior's word is final
I am resurrected
Blood-protected
I am a miracle child
I've been crucified
Raised with Christ
I am a miracle child

Source: LyricFind
Songwriters: Brandon Lake/Ethan Hulse/Jacob Sooter
Miracle Child lyrics Essential Music Publishing

Resource List

Brain Injury Association of America
https://www.biausa.org/brain-injury/about-brain-i
njury/nbiic/contact-nbiic#:~:text=You%20may%20spe
ak,find%20your%20BIA.

Brain Injury Association of America
3057 Nutley Street #805
Fairfax, VA 22031-1931
info@biausa.org
703-761-0750
703-761-0755

Brain Injury Association of America – Texas Division
P.O. Box 95234
Grapevine, TX 76099
www.biausa.org/Texas
For brain injury information, personal assistance in identi-
fying brain injury

programs and related services, and information about support groups,

please contact the BIAA-TX Brain Injury Information Center

toll-free at 1-800-444-6443.Texas Brain Injury Association

The Texas Health and Human Services (HHS) Office of

Acquired Brain Injury (OABI) is the only state agency specifically focused on brain injury prevention, treatment, and education.
Website: https://hhs.texas.gov/services/disability/office-acquired-brain-injury
Email: OABI@hhsc.state.tx.us
Phone: 512-706-7191

Pate Rehabilitation Corporate Office
8222 N. Beltline Road, Suite 175
Irving, Texas 75063
Pate Rehabilitation serves people with brain injuries, their families, and the community at large by providing professional services, support, and education that is focused on returning injured individuals to their highest possible level of independence and quality of life.

Every March, the Brain Injury Association of America (BIAA) leads the nation in observing Brain Injury Awareness Month. This year, we have exciting new developments for the brain injury community, including a new awareness campaign, advocacy initiatives, events, fundraising opportunities, new publications, and more.

About the author

A small town situated around fifty miles from Dallas, Corsicana, Texas was Dee Dee's birthplace in 1950. Born Adalia Kamp, after being taken home to siblings who could not handle the pronunciation, she became Dee Dee, which was her lifetime preference. Rather poor but raised with high hopes and dreams. Church provided a social environment, but Mom taught her about godly expectations. She defined her own ambitions and never hesitated to put in the hard work needed to achieve them.

She developed fortitude through two marriages, owning a design center, and fostering impressive professional capabilities. With a fulfilling career at AT&T, spanning twenty-two years, she realized her dream of working in the aviation department and dispatching company jets. Dee Dee appreciated the company standing behind her as she prioritized her commitments. She still loves AT&T.

The birth of her son, Andy, was the pinnacle of her achievements. Placing him in a godly position, she idolized him. She learned through almost losing her son that she needed God above anyone or anything. Dee Dee learned how to pray, how to create an authentic relationship with God, how to believe in healing, and how to rely on God's timing.

She answered the call from her Lord to write this book and give hope to others during their trials and tribulations.

Dee Dee and Andy now enjoy a grateful life in Granbury, Texas, attending the Heights Church with many wonderful, dedicated prayer warriors and friends.

A Mother's Thoughts

A Mother and Son's bond
Remains a special one
It remains strong
Through many years
It is an amazing gift from God
                    --Dee Dee Ward

Coming Soon

If you enjoyed our story, a shorter version was accepted for publication *Stories of Roaring Faith: Volume 6* coming from Roaring Lambs in the near future. www.RoaringLam bs.org. This series of anthologies contains testimonies from numerous authors that will help build your faith.

As for Dee Dee, she plans to continue writing.

Andy and Dee Dee can be reached by email: Warddeedee 33@gmail.com